MATE WITH
"THE SHIP THAT HELD THE LINE"

LEGENDS OF WARFARE
NAVAL

USS Hornet (CV-8)
From the Doolittle Raid and Midway to Santa Cruz

DAVID DOYLE

SCHIFFER MILITARY

4880 Lower Valley Road   Atglen, PA 19310

Designed by Justin Watkinson
Technical Layout by Jack Chappell
Type set in Impact/Minion Pro/Univers LT Std

ISBN: 978-0-7643-5862-3
Printed in China

Published by Schiffer Publishing, Ltd.
4880 Lower Valley Road
Atglen, PA 19310
Phone: (610) 593-1777; Fax: (610) 593-2002
E-mail: Info@schifferbooks.com
www.schifferbooks.com

For our complete selection of fine books on this and related subjects, please visit our website at www.schifferbooks.com. You may also write for a free catalog.

Schiffer Publishing's titles are available at special discounts for bulk purchases for sales promotions or premiums. Special editions, including personalized covers, corporate imprints, and excerpts, can be created in large quantities for special needs. For more information, contact the publisher.

We are always looking for people to write books on new and related subjects. If you have an idea for a book, please contact us at proposals@schifferbooks.com.

Acknowledgments

When the United States was drawn into World War II, USS *Hornet* was the newest of a new type of capital ship—the aircraft carrier. The ship would last only a week beyond the first anniversary of its commissioning, but during that year not only would it steam into the history books as the launching place of Col. Jimmy Doolittle's raid on Tokyo, but it also would for a time be America's only operational aircraft carrier in the Pacific.

This volume can but scratch the surface of the individual heroism shown by the men who served aboard and flew from the *Hornet*, but it will showcase their ship—the vessel that was at once their home, their workplace, and their lifeline.

The materials contained in these pages were compiled from the records of the US Navy, the National Museum of Naval Aviation, the Naval History and Heritage Command, the National Museum of the United States Air Force, and the National Archives and Records Administration.

In compiling this history I was truly blessed to have the invaluable help of many colleagues that I am fortunate to call my friends, including Tom Kailbourn, Scott Taylor, Sean Hert, Tracy White, James Noblin, Dave Baker, Rick Davis, and Dana Bell. Their generous and skillful assistance adds immensely to the quality of this volume. I am especially blessed to have the ongoing help of my wonderful wife, Denise, who has scanned thousands of photos and documents for this and numerous other books. Beyond that, she is an ongoing source of support and inspiration.

All photos are from the collections of the US National Archives and Records Administration unless otherwise noted.

Contents

Introduction

While Japan and China clashed in the Marco Polo Bridge incident in July 1937, and France, fearing an attack by Germany, reinforced the Maginot Line, a brand new warship was undergoing trials in the serene waters of Chesapeake Bay. The Newport News Shipbuilding and Dry Dock Company's latest creation, the 20,000-ton carrier *Yorktown* was the first of her class of what was destined to be three sisters. In September it would be turned over to the Navy for commissioning, becoming USS *Yorktown*, the first truly battle-worthy, purpose-built aircraft carrier of the US Navy. At pier side, her near-identical sister ship the *Enterprise* was in the final stages of fitting out.

While these ships were sleek and modern, indeed the most-able aircraft carriers in the Navy's arsenal, their 1933 design, limited by terms of the Washington Naval Treaty, was less than ideal. The Navy wanted larger carriers, with larger flight decks and greater hangar space—as well as better armor protection—all things that could not be achieved within the prohibitions imposed by the treaty.

By fiscal year 1938, with the world situation demanding that the Navy add another aircraft carrier to its fleet, the nation was no longer bound by the treaty-specified weight limits. However, other limits came into play. A global conflict had begun, and, fearing that the United States would be drawn into this, teams of naval architects and draftsmen were hurriedly designing new 45,000-ton battleships (the *Iowa* class). The engineering manpower was simply not available to complete a new aircraft carrier design.

Accordingly, the decision was made to request authorization to construct a third *Yorktown*-class carrier with only modest revisions in the design. The third carrier would be named *Hornet*. The request was made, and the Naval Expansion Act of May 1938 provided the authorization and the funding.

The new ship would have fewer portholes than its elder sisters, as well as a revised bridge, and would utilize Mk. 37 directors for its 5-inch dual-purpose guns rather than the Mk. 33 directors of its predecessors.

USS *Hornet* Data

Ordered	March 30, 1939
Laid down	September 25, 1939
Launched	December 14, 1940
Commissioned	October 20, 1941
Sunk	October 27, 1942
Stricken	January 13, 1943
Builder	Newport News Shipbuilding & Dry Dock Co.
Class	*Yorktown*
Sponsor	Anne Reid (Mrs. Frank) Knox

Displacement, Standard	19,900 tons
Displacement, Full Load	25,600 tons
Length, waterline, full load	770 feet
Length, hull	809 feet 9 inches
Length, flight deck	816 feet
Length, overall	824 feet 9 inches
Beam, waterline, full load	83 feet 2½ inches
Beam, maximum	109 feet 6¼ inches
Design draft	24 feet
Bunker fuel	4,280 tons
Endurance (design)	12,500 nautical miles @ 15 knots
Boilers	9 Babcock and Wilcox, 400 psi
Machinery	4 Parsons geared turbines, 120,000 total shaft horsepower
Speed	32.5 knots
Armor	4"–2.5" belt; 60 lbs. protective deck(s); 4" bulkheads; 4" (side)–2" (top) conning tower; 4" (side) over steering gear
Armament, as built	8 single 5"/38-caliber gun mounts; 4 quad 1.1"/75-caliber machine gun mounts; 24 .50-caliber machine guns
Armament, January 1942	8 single 5"/38-caliber gun mounts; 4 quad 1.1"/75-caliber machine gun mounts; 30 20 mm Oerlikon guns; 18 .50-caliber machine guns
Radar (starting in October 1940)	SC, later also fitted with CXAM
Aircraft:	72
Aviation gasoline	177,950 gallons
Aviation facilities	3 elevators; 2 flight-deck and 1 hangar-deck hydraulic catapults

Crew in 1941: ship 86 officers, 1,280 enlisted; air wing 141 officers, 710 enlisted

Originally, the *Yorktown* class was supposed to consist of only these two ships, *Yorktown* (right) and *Enterprise* (left), seen here in February 1937 as the ships are being fitted out by their builder, Newport News Shipbuilding and Dry Dock Company. However, the deteriorating world condition led Congress to authorize a third such ship, the *Hornet*, in 1938.

CHAPTER 1
Construction

The construction of any naval vessel is a complex proposition, and for a vessel the size of the *Hornet*, especially so. That said, because the *Hornet* would essentially duplicate the earlier *Yorktown* and *Enterprise* and was being built in the same shipyard, the process was eased. Further, the world situation, especially U-boats prowling off the US coast, added a sense of urgency to the shipyard workers.

The keel for the new carrier was laid at Newport News Shipbuilding and Dry Dock Company on September 25, 1939. Just under fifteen months later, ship's sponsor (and wife of the secretary of the US Navy) Annie Reid Knox smashed the customary bottle of champagne on the bulbous bow of the ship, sending it sliding down the builder's ways into the sea.

Just as both *Yorktown* and *Enterprise* took under two years each to finish to the launching stage, versus the fifteen months of *Hornet*, so too was *Hornet*'s fitting out and commissioning accelerated. Only ten months after launching (versus about a year and a half for each of its sisters), *Hornet* was ready for commissioning.

When the *Hornet* slid down the ways and into the water, though imposing looking the ship was far from complete. In fact, at launch she was little more than an empty hull with machinery in place. In the following ten months that hull was transformed into a ship, as yard workers threaded miles of wiring through the ship. Plumbing was installed for the galley and the numerous restrooms (heads) needed by thousands of men. Communication equipment, stoves, desks, ammunition hoists, laundry equipment, refrigeration plants, and the myriad of other appliances needed for everyday life, as well as for waging war, were securely bolted in place.

Just as the ship itself was coming together, so too was the crew. Named to take command of the ship was Capt. Marc A. Mitscher, who, in 1919, had been awarded the Navy Cross for his part in the first transatlantic flight by naval aviators.

Prior to receiving orders to *Hornet*, Mitscher had been assistant chief of the Navy's Bureau of Aeronautics. These experiences provided Mitscher with a commanding knowledge of those most capable in the naval aviation community, knowledge he put to use in requesting officers to fill the billets aboard his new command. About half the enlisted men crewing the carrier were experienced sailors, some with decades of service, while the other half comprised new seamen, freshly arriving from their boot camp—the Great Lakes Naval Training Station near Chicago.

With the crew in place, *Hornet* was ready to join the fleet. On October 20, 1941, Secretary of the Navy Frank Knox addressed those on hand for the commissioning ceremony, reminding those assembled that only three days earlier the destroyer USS *Kearny* had been torpedoed by a German U-boat, with eleven men killed. After the Secretary concluded his remarks, Mitscher stepped forward and following the time-honored traditions of the US Navy, read his orders of command and took command of the ship, which now had the prefix USS (United States Ship) before her name.

U.S.S. HORNET (CV8)
KEEL LAYING
N.N.S.&D.D.Co
1939, SEP. 25-TH.

H-385-No.1
9-25-39

The keel of the eighth US Navy aircraft carrier, which would be commissioned USS *Hornet* (CV-8), was laid on September 25, 1939, at the Newport News Shipbuilding and Dry Dock Company, Newport News, Virginia. It was the sixth US warship to bear the name *Hornet* and was the third and last carrier in the *Yorktown* class. This photo was taken on the day of the keel laying, the ceremony marking the official commencement of construction (from above the bow, facing aft).

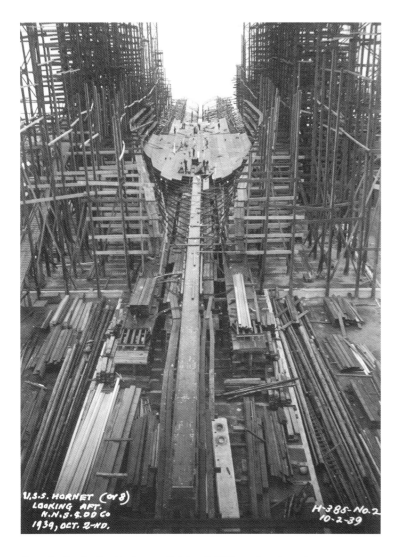

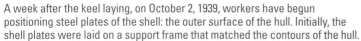

A week after the keel laying, on October 2, 1939, workers have begun positioning steel plates of the shell: the outer surface of the hull. Initially, the shell plates were laid on a support frame that matched the contours of the hull.

The progress of the *Hornet*'s hull is viewed from aft on the building ways at Newport News on October 2, 1939. Note how the support frames for the stern are anchored underwater, to the rear of the building ways. Wooden staging to the sides of the hull will support planks for workers as the construction of the ship advances.

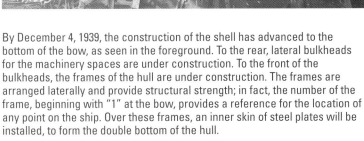

By December 4, 1939, the construction of the shell has advanced to the bottom of the bow, as seen in the foreground. To the rear, lateral bulkheads for the machinery spaces are under construction. To the front of the bulkheads, the frames of the hull are under construction. The frames are arranged laterally and provide structural strength; in fact, the number of the frame, beginning with "1" at the bow, provides a reference for the location of any point on the ship. Over these frames, an inner skin of steel plates will be installed, to form the double bottom of the hull.

In another December 4, 1939, photograph, the stern is in the foreground, showing the shape of the skeg on the lower aft part of the hull. Farther forward, frame members are being constructed on top of the shell, and the bulkheads of the machinery spaces are in the background.

By February 1, 1940, construction of the *Hornet*, as seen from the front of the hull, had advanced to the point that there were several levels amidships. Lateral beams have been installed amidships to support a deck; some of the deck plates are in place, with rectangular openings in them for the uptakes from the boilers to the smokestack.

The *Hornet* is viewed from amidships facing aft on February 1, 1940, showing several of the lateral bulkheads. Farther aft, several large frame members are under construction: note the oblong lightening holes in them.

This is a reverse view of the preceding photo, taken on the same date, February 1, 1940, facing forward and showing workmen in the foreground assembling frame members in the stern. In the background is the multilevel bulkhead at the rear of the machinery spaces. The idea of this massive box-within-the-hull structure was to give protection to the vulnerable machinery and systems in the center of the hull.

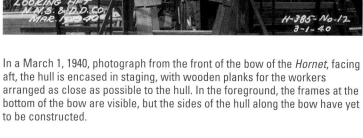

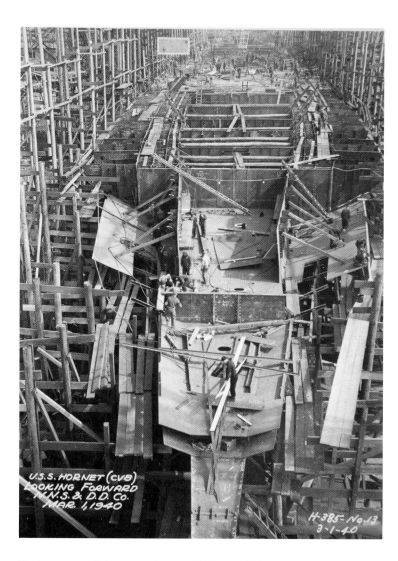

In a March 1, 1940, photograph from the front of the bow of the *Hornet*, facing aft, the hull is encased in staging, with wooden planks for the workers arranged as close as possible to the hull. In the foreground, the frames at the bottom of the bow are visible, but the sides of the hull along the bow have yet to be constructed.

The lower part of the narrow bottom of the stern is in the foreground of this March 1, 1940, photo. Wooden braces propped against the shell plates in the middle background are being used to support two longitudinal bulkheads.

Some progress has been made on the construction of the bow of the *Hornet* in this April 2, 1940, photograph. Since the March 1 photo from a similar perspective was taken, further construction had been done amidships, with more bulkheads being erected.

The compartment with the pointed rear bulkhead in the foreground of this April 2, 1940, photo, taken above the stern of the *Hornet*, would become the steering-gear room. The compartment immediately forward of the steering-gear room would be the motor and control room. The spaces in the hull to each side of these two compartments would be voids.

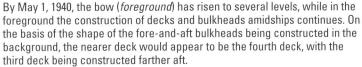

By May 1, 1940, the bow (*foreground*) has risen to several levels, while in the foreground the construction of decks and bulkheads amidships continues. On the basis of the shape of the fore-and-aft bulkheads being constructed in the background, the nearer deck would appear to be the fourth deck, with the third deck being constructed farther aft.

The hull of the *Hornet* is viewed from the stern looking forward in a May 1, 1940, photograph. Note the curved frame members on both sides of the hull in the foreground, to which similarly curved shell plates later will be attached.

By July 1, 1940, construction of the forward part of the hull was well underway; in the foreground is the second deck. Farther aft, lateral bulkheads are being installed on this same deck.

On the same date, July 1, 1940, the progress of construction is documented from above the aft part of the hull, facing forward. In the foreground is the third deck, with the second deck, with plating installed, farther forward. As with other capital ships, construction of the hull tended to proceed more intensively amidships than in the bow and stern.

The carrier *Hornet* is observed from above the aft part of the hull on August 1, 1940, with the second deck visible in the foreground. From the bulkhead forward, most of the steel plates for the hangar deck, also called the main deck, are in place. The two curved deck plates in the foreground delineate the forward corners of the opening for elevator number 3. Amidships, the opening for elevator 2 is visible; this elevator was to the starboard of the centerline of the ship.

A month after the two preceding photos, construction continues on the second deck, as seen from the bow, facing aft, on August 1, 1940. Some of the frame members have been installed in the foreground; the nearest one is frame 11, and this will form an arch over a crew berthing space. The area closer to the bow will be for boatswain's stores.

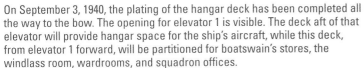
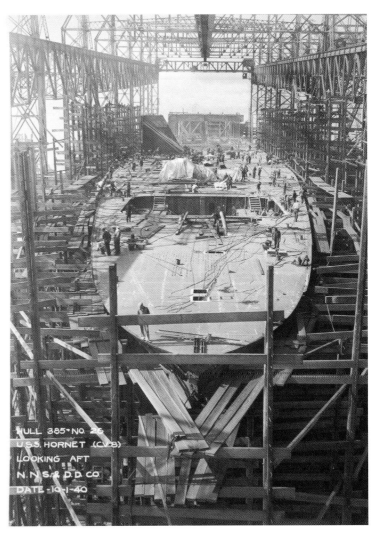

On September 3, 1940, the plating of the hangar deck has been completed all the way to the bow. The opening for elevator 1 is visible. The deck aft of that elevator will provide hangar space for the ship's aircraft, while this deck, from elevator 1 forward, will be partitioned for boatswain's stores, the windlass room, wardrooms, and squadron offices.

From a similar perspective to that of the preceding photo (taken on September 3, 1940), the hangar deck in the foreground remains little changed as of October 1, except for the cutting of two new hatches in the foreground. Amidships, some of the frames and bulkheads for the cavernous hangar have been positioned.

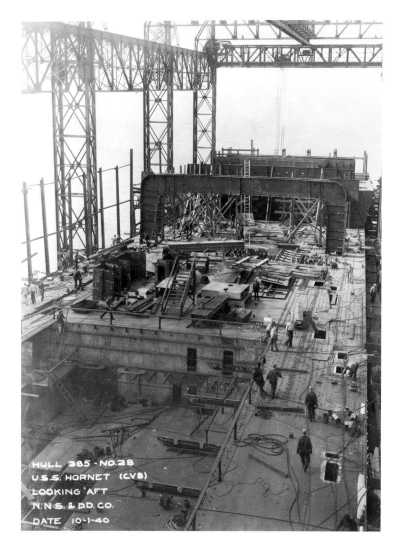

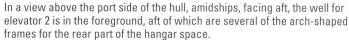

In a view above the port side of the hull, amidships, facing aft, the well for elevator 2 is in the foreground, aft of which are several of the arch-shaped frames for the rear part of the hangar space.

Taken on the same date as the preceding photo, October 1, 1940, this view is from farther aft, facing forward, showing the same arch-shaped frames seen in the preceding photos. In the foreground is a watertight bulkhead at frame 186; to the immediate front of that bulkhead is the well for elevator 3.

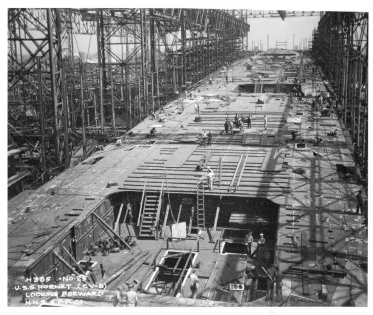

This undated photograph of the *Hornet*'s flight deck was taken from above the well for elevator 3 sometime after November 1, 1940, at which time only the flight deck was framed, but before December 2, by which time the flight deck had been plated and the island was under construction.

By November 1, 1940, the framing for the flight deck was in place, as seen from above the aft starboard part of the hull. The flight deck of the *Hornet* would be planked over with Douglas fir and would not be armored.

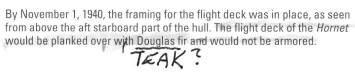

TEAK?

U.S.S. NO. 32
U.S.S. HORNET (CV8)
LOOKING AFT
N.N.S. & D.D CO.
DATE 12-2-40

The bow ramp—the rolled front edge of the flight deck—of the *Hornet* is of interest in this December 2, 1940, photograph, taken twelve days before the launching of the ship. Below the front of the flight deck is a catwalk walkway, and below that a temporary structure used while building the flight deck. Between the forecastle deck and the flight deck was the gallery deck, the front of which is in the shadow below the flight deck.

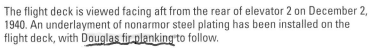

The flight deck is viewed facing aft from the rear of elevator 2 on December 2, 1940. An underlayment of nonarmor steel plating has been installed on the flight deck, with Douglas fir planking to follow.

This elevated view facing forward from above and aft of the well for elevator 3 was taken on December 2, 1940. On the starboard side of the flight deck amidships, the island is under construction.

H-385
USS HORNET (CV8)
LOOKING QUARTER BOW
N.N.S. + D.D. CO.
NO. 35   1-18-41

Hornet is viewed off her port bow on January 18, 1941. Draft markings, white numbers for visually assessing the vertical measurement from the waterline to the keel, are painted on the bow. Not readily noticeable is the fact that the frame numbers were painted in small, white numerals just above the boot topping, the black band around the waterline of the hull.

H-385
U.S.S. HORNET (CV8)
LOOKING QUARTER STERN
N.N.S. & D.D. Co.
No. 36   1-18-41

The carrier *Hornet* is viewed off her aft port quarter at its fitting-out dock at Newport News Shipbuilding and Dry Dock Company on January 18, 1941, four days after her launching. During the fitting-out period, the construction of the ship would continue until its commissioning day, when the ship would be transferred to the US Navy. Note the scaffolding around the island and the tripod mast with two platforms. The upper one was for antiaircraft machine guns and sky lookouts, and the lower one was for antiaircraft fire control.

Thirteen days after the preceding photo was taken, this one was snapped from a similar perspective on January 31, 1941. In both photos, the forward end of the belt armor is visible. Ranging from 2.5 to 4 inches in thickness, the belt armor was applied in a strip above and below the waterline to provide some protection from torpedoes along the most-vital parts of the hull. The front of the belt armor is at frame 35 and is easily discernible by its light color, contrasting with the black of the boot topping.

Workmen stand on scaffolding just above the armored belt, apparently welding steel plates over the openings that had originally provided for portholes.

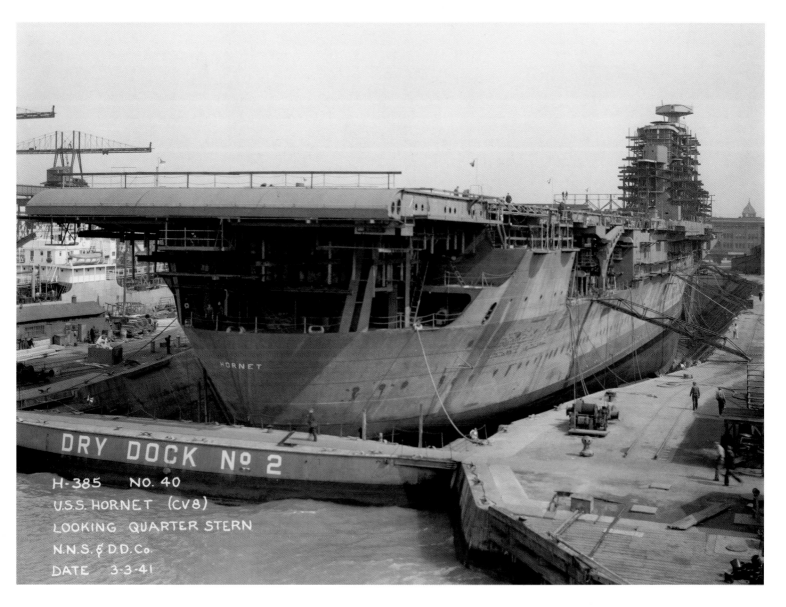

Within the photo:

DRY DOCK Nº 2

H-385   NO. 40
U.S.S. HORNET (CV8)
LOOKING QUARTER STERN
N.N.S. & D.D.Co.
DATE 3-3-41

HORNET

Hornet is observed from astern in drydock 2 on March 3, 1941, showing the rolled surface of the stern ramp of the flight deck, as well as the support frames from the fantail to the bottom of the rear of the flight deck. Some of the structures visible above the fantail are temporary staging for the workers.

By April 1, 1941, the *Hornet* had returned to its fitting-out dock at Newport News; it is seen here on that date from off the port bow. The two diagonal objects running from the port side of the forecastle deck up to the underside of the flight deck were temporary braces.

H-385   NO. 41
U.S.S. HORNET (CV8)
LOOKING QUART. PORT BOW
N.N.S. & D.D.CO.
DATE 4-1-41

H-385   NO. 42
U.S.S. HORNET (CV8)
LOOKING QUART. STB. STERN
N.N.S. & D.D.CO.
DATE 4-1-41

On April 1, 1941, *Hornet* is viewed from the aft starboard quarter. Scaffolding still encloses the island. Note the boat crane in the open bay on the hangar deck between the stern and the island.

On May 1, 1941, the carrier is seen from the forward starboard quarter as the fitting-out continues.

The *Hornet* is observed from the aft starboard quarter at Newport News on May 1, 1941. On the dock is a crane for hoisting components and equipment up to the carrier.

On June 2, 1941, considerable staging planks were still suspended along the hull of the *Hornet*.

HULL 385   NO. 45
U.S.S. HORNET (CV8)
LOOKING QTR. PORT BOW
N.N.S. & D.D. CO.
DATE. 6-2-41.

HULL 385   NO. 46
U.S.S. HORNET (CV8)
LOOKING QTR. PORT STERN
N.N.S. & D.D. CO.
DATE. 6-2-41

The *Hornet* is seen from its aft port quarter on June 2, 1941. Much of the staging had been removed from around the island, revealing more of its structure. The ship was equipped with two Mk. 37 directors for controlling its antiaircraft gun batteries; the aft Mk. 37 director is the turret-shaped structure on the upper rear of the island.

Smoke is issuing from the smokestack of the *Hornet* on July 1, 1941, indicating perhaps that the boilers were being tested.

H-385   NO. 47
U.S.S. HORNET   (CV8)
LOOKING: QUARTER BOW - (PORT)
N.N.S.& D.D.CO.
DATE: 7-1-41

Three of the *Hornet*'s boats have been brought aboard, and they are secured in bays on the hangar deck. Typically, on the port side of the *Yorktown*-class carriers, *from front to rear*, a 35-foot motorboat, a 40-foot motorboat admiral's barge, and a 50-foot motor launch with a 26-foot motor whaleboat nested in it were carried.

H-385   NO. 48
U.S.S. HORNET   (CV8)
LOOKING: QUARTER STERN (PORT)
N.N.S.& D.D.CO.
DATE: 7-1-41

Less than three months before its commissioning, the *Hornet* was photographed from off its port bow on August 4, 1941. The boats had been removed from this side of the carrier, and much of the staging around the island had been stripped away. Visible on the front end of the island are the Mk. 37 director above the pilothouse, the open bridge around the front and sides of the pilothouse, and primary fly control (nicknamed "pri-fly"): the booth with rectangular windows on the side of the island just aft of the pilothouse.

H-385   No. 49
U.S.S. HORNET (CV8)
LOOKING : QUARTER BOW (PORT)
N.N.S. & D.D. Co.
DATE: 8-4-41.

Later on the same date the preceding photo was taken, August 4, 1941, repainting of the hull had begun, advancing as far as amidships. At the time of its commissioning in October, the ship wore a Measure 12 camouflage scheme, with Sea Blue (5-S) from the boot topping up to the hangar deck, Ocean Gray (5-O) from the hangar deck to the top of the superstructure (in this case, the smokestack), and Haze Gray (5-H) on any structures above the superstructure.

The freshly painted *Hornet* is observed from off its port bow at Newport News on September 2, 1941. Since August 4, the yardarm had been added to the foretop on the tripod mast. In this photo, there is still staging around the foretop. Faintly visible above the pilothouse and to the front of the forward Mk. 37 director is a rangefinder, which was installed in May or June.

As seen in a September 2, 1941, photo from the aft port quarter of *Hornet*, side ladders have been installed forward and amidships. Two boat booms had been mounted on the hull since early August. These are the diagonal, pole-shaped objects forward and aft of the boat crane. Boat booms were designed to swing out from the hull so that boats could be moored to it while the ship was at anchor. In the preceding photo, the forward boat boom is visible to the front of the forward roller-door opening of the hangar deck; this boom is positioned upright, has not yet been installed on its swivel mount, and is surrounded by staging.

The *Hornet* returned to drydock at Newport News in September 1941; this bow-on photo was taken on the seventeenth. Note the two ring-shaped bow chocks on the forecastle, the two anchors, and the gallery walkway, about 4 feet below the sides and the front of the flight deck.

H-385   Nº 57
HORNET   (CV-8)
BOW-LOOKING AFT
(IN DRY DOCK)
N.N.S.& D.D.CO.
DATE: 9-17-41

On the same date as the preceding photo, the bow of the *Hornet* is seen from a higher perspective. A very close inspection of the original photograph reveals that inclining experiments were being conducted on this date. These experiments, intended to calculate the vertical center of gravity of the ship and other essential data, were conducted by moving several large weights mounted on temporary tracks back and forth on the flight deck and measuring changes in the angle of the ship. One set of these tracks and weights is visible on the flight deck to the front of the island.

Details of the forecastle deck and the starboard side of the hull are apparent in this September 17, 1941, photograph. When a ship such as *Hornet* is placed in drydock, the hull rests on large blocks on the floor of the dock, and it is imperative to very carefully position those blocks, or the hull can suffer severe damage. Scattered on the floor of the drydock are additional blocks for use with other ships.

The lower rear of the hull is observed from the starboard side in drydock on September 17, 1941, showing the two starboard propellers, shafts, and shaft struts, as well as the rudder. On the side of the hull to the right is the aft starboard boat boom, the aft end of which is secured to a tripod-shaped travel lock. Below the boom is stenciled "PROPELLER / KEEP CLEAR" above a downward-pointing arrow.

With only eighteen days remaining before its commissioning, the *Hornet* rests along the fitting-out dock at Newport News on October 2, 1941. The contrast in the shades of the Measure 12 camouflage paint colors, Ocean Gray above the hangar deck, and Sea Blue below the hangar deck, is apparent; this demarcation between the colors is in line with the hawse pipe that the shank of the anchor is secured in.

The demarcation between the upper Ocean Gray and lower Sea Blue paint colors is visible along the line of the hangar deck in this view of the *Hornet* from astern on October 2, 1941. A 36-foot motor launch is stored on the aft end of the forecastle deck, below the rear of the flight deck. Two platforms below the aft ramp of the flight deck—a small one on the port side and a larger one at the center—were for the use of crewmen while raising and lowering the pivoting flagstaff mounted on the aft ramp.

As seen in an October 13, 1941, photograph of the starboard side of the *Hornet*, facing aft, the cylindrical structure to the front of the island, below the pilothouse, was a tub for the director for the number 2 1.1-inch quadruple (quad) antiaircraft machine gun mount. Note the door on the first level of the forward-starboard facet of this tub. Five motorboats and launches are stored alongside the island.

Hornet is observed from its starboard side at the fitting-out pier at Newport News around the time of its commissioning in October 1941, providing an idea of the framing under various platforms from the foretop down to the hangar deck. Two whaleboats are suspended from cables on the underside of the gallery deck, below the island.

The forward part of the island of the *Hornet* is viewed from below on the starboard side in or around October 1941, showing the navigating bridge, the foretop, a boat crane, and a motorboat.

With one week to go until commissioning, the *Hornet* is viewed from above the forward end of the flight deck on October 13, 1941. The ship's identification code, "HNT," is painted on the forward end of the flight deck.

On October 13, 1941, with work on the *Hornet* nearly completed, a painter is touching up the flight deck. Note the fully rigged tripod foremast and mainmast, the latter being attached to the rear of the smokestack.

The arrestor cables on the flight deck are seen from the aft port corner of the deck in another October 13, 1941, photo. In the foreground is elevator 3, around which is its guardrail, which is raised a few inches. When the elevator was lowered, this guardrail was fully raised. Running across the deck every few feet are tie-down strips: metal strips with C-shaped openings in them for attaching stays to aircraft.

The hangar deck of the *Hornet* is seen facing aft around the time of its commissioning. To the right is an open bay; this bay and the other ones on this deck could be closed off by an overhead rolling curtain. In the left background is a housing for the uptakes, bomb elevators, and work and storage spaces. The rise near the camera leads from the hanger deck to the hanger deck catapult, which is located at the apex of the rise.

On October 20, 1941—two years and one month after its keel was laid—the *Hornet* was commissioned. At this point, the ship began active service with the US Navy and gained the designation "USS" (United States Ship) before its name. Secretary of the Navy Frank Knox, at the podium, addressed the gathered company at the commissioning ceremony at Newport News.

Guests and naval officers are dining on USS *Hornet* on the day of her commissioning. Secretary Knox is at the head of the nearer table.

CHAPTER 2
Into Service

USS *Hornet* is steaming off Norfolk, Virginia, on the date of its commissioning, October 20, 1941. The ship exhibits her original Measure 12 camouflage scheme.

Standard practice of the time would have had *Hornet* sail for the coast of Maine for a series of trials once it was commissioned, but with U-boats lurking off the coast and with the military mindful of the recent torpedoing of the *Kearny*, the Navy opted to keep *Hornet* in the safety of Chesapeake Bay for her speed runs and trials. The risk of the new, untried carrier being at sea when the nation seemed on the cusp of war was too great.

By November, the ship had finally been equipped with her 5-inch/38-caliber, dual-purpose guns. These weapons were designed for use both against aircraft and surface targets, such as enemy warships and submarines operating on the surface. Each of these eight weapons, installed on open, single-base ring mounts just below the flight deck, could hurl a 53-pound shell 18,000 yards against surface targets, or up to 37,200 feet at 85-degree elevation when firing at aircraft. Its speed of firing was rated at fifteen rounds per minute, but in the hands of a well-trained crew, upward of twenty rounds per minute could be sustained for brief periods of time.

Early December 1941 found *Hornet* continuing to operate out of Norfolk Naval Base, training crew and further refining the operation of the ship. The morning of December 7 saw her tied peacefully at Pier 4, with many of her crew ashore on leave, including her captain.

Hornet's radioman received reports that Pearl Harbor had been attacked by the Japanese; these were soon followed by official notification of the attack, and that the ship was to make preparation for combat. The captain and the executive officer were summoned to the ship, and soon the remainder of the crew were as well.

Two days before Christmas 1941, the true armament of the carrier started coming aboard, as hundreds of aviation ordnance men, mechanics, and parachute riggers boarded the ship. Two days after Christmas, with *Hornet* at sea, the pilots of Air Group 8 began landing their Wildcats, dive bombers, and Devastators aboard the ship, and at last *Hornet* truly became an aircraft carrier.

A monthlong training cruise in the Gulf of Mexico honed the men and their ship into a single, cohesive entity. On January 30, 1942, *Hornet* returned to Norfolk for repairs of the minor problems that had been exposed during the training cruise, and, it was believed, to give the crew some leave. However, while there, the stage was being set for what would be her greatest exploit.

On February 2, *Hornet* made preparations to get under way. Crewmen working on the flight deck, hangar, or island had a view of a peculiar sight. Two US Army B-25 Mitchell twin-engine medium bombers were taxiing from the airfield to the carrier pier. *Hornet*'s heavy aircraft crane gently lifted them aboard, in an operation that was deliberately omitted from *Hornet*'s logs and other documentation, and shortly thereafter the carrier cast off and put to sea.

Early in the afternoon, one of the bombers was spotted adjacent to the island, in a position comparable to where it would be if fifteen of the aircraft were on the flight deck. At 1:27 p.m., Lt. John E. Fitzgerald, a test pilot previously assigned to Wright Field, took off in a B-25 loaded with sandbags to simulate a partial bombload. Later that afternoon, Lt. James F. McCarthy used 275 feet of *Hornet*'s flight deck to get airborne in a B-25 laden with sandbags simulating a full bombload. With the concept of launching B-25s from the carrier having been proven, *Hornet* returned to Norfolk, where it would remain until March. During that time it would be repainted into the Measure 12 (Modified) camouflage scheme that substituted 5-N Navy Blue for the 5-S Sea Blue of her original camouflage, and the breaking up of the straight lines with splotches of the different colors extending up and down from their original boundaries.

The *Hornet* is viewed from another perspective. The foremast was painted Haze Gray from the level of the top of the smokestack up. The top of the smokestack and the mainmast were painted a dark color, evidently black. *National Museum of Naval Aviation*

An aerial photo taken on *Hornet*'s christening day catches the ship off her aft port quarter. A boat is stored in each of the three aft bays of the hangar deck.

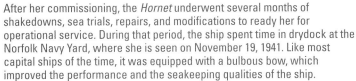

After her commissioning, the *Hornet* underwent several months of shakedowns, sea trials, repairs, and modifications to ready her for operational service. During that period, the ship spent time in drydock at the Norfolk Navy Yard, where she is seen on November 19, 1941. Like most capital ships of the time, it was equipped with a bulbous bow, which improved the performance and the seakeeping qualities of the ship.

In this remarkable, low-angle image taken while *Hornet* was in drydock at Norfolk Navy Yard in November 1941, workmen on staging planks suspended by ropes from hooks attached to the hull are scraping rust and loose paint from the shell—an essential part of the drydocking of any ship.

Inside the photograph:

OFFICIAL PHOTOGRAPH
TO BE RELEASED FOR PUBLICATION

HORNET

H-385   No. 67.
U.S.S. HORNET (CV 8)
(AFTER COMMISSIONING)
STERN-LOOKING FORWARD.
NORFOLK NAVY YARD.
DATE: 11-19-41.

The layout of the plates that comprise the shell around the stern of the *Hornet* is prominent in this photo taken in drydock at Norfolk Navy Yard on November 19, 1941.

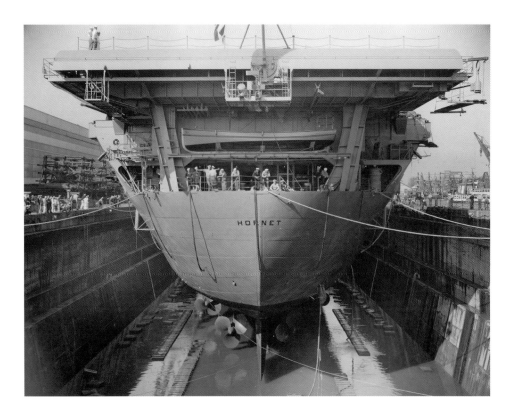

In another of the views of the *Hornet* in drydock in November 1941, in this light and from this angle it is clear that the draft marks on both sides of the stern were slightly raised, with paint applied, instead of being simply painted onto the shell. Note that the swiveling flagstaff on the center of the aft ramp of the flight deck is raised and its two braces are secured.

The three-bladed propellers, the propeller-shaft struts, and the rudder are in view in this photo taken under the stern of the *Hornet* in drydock at Norfolk Navy Yard. The propeller blades were not of an uninterrupted rounded shape; they had facets, somewhat like a pentagon with rounded corners.

The two port propellers were photographed during *Hornet*'s drydocking at Norfolk Navy Yard in November 1941. Visible in the distance below the bend in the hull are two bilge keels. These finlike structures were used in pairs on each side of the hull to reduce the ship's proclivity to roll.

The rudder is viewed from the port side in drydock. On the side of the fin upon which the rudder is mounted are light-colored zinc strips, which acted as anodes to counteract galvanic corrosion to the rudder and its mount.

On the side of the hull on the boot topping (the black band around the waterline of the ship), above the port outboard propeller, is a visible, vertical irregularity in the surface. This is the rear terminus of the belt armor, affixed over the shell. The curved bottom of the belt armor is visible along the hull. The aft port boat boom is casting a large shadow on the side of the hull.

The port side of the aft part of the hull is viewed from farther forward than in the preceding photo, permitting a view of the two portside bilge keels. A few yards above the bilge keels is the long shadow cast by the bottom of the belt armor.

Sailors are scraping and prepping the port side of the lower hull of the *Hornet* for priming and painting. The staging planks they are standing on are suspended by ropes, which are connected, via S-hooks, to eyes permanently affixed to the shell of the hull for this purpose.

A final view of sailors scraping the lower hull of the *Hornet* was taken along the port side; the forward port boat boom, also seen in the preceding photo, is to the upper left of the photo.

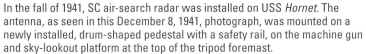

In the fall of 1941, SC air-search radar was installed on USS *Hornet*. The antenna, as seen in this December 8, 1941, photograph, was mounted on a newly installed, drum-shaped pedestal with a safety rail, on the machine gun and sky-lookout platform at the top of the tripod foremast.

Also installed on the *Hornet* in the fall of 1941 was a BI radar antenna. As seen in this December 8, 1941, photograph, the BI radar antenna was mounted on the forward part of the fire-control platform on the tripod foremast.

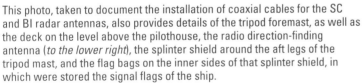

This photo, taken to document the installation of coaxial cables for the SC and BI radar antennas, also provides details of the tripod foremast, as well as the deck on the level above the pilothouse, the radio direction-finding antenna (*to the lower right*), the splinter shield around the aft legs of the tripod mast, and the flag bags on the inner sides of that splinter shield, in which were stored the signal flags of the ship.

In a compartment adjacent to the radar plot was the SC radar compartment. The transmitter for this radar is to the right, above which is a passing scuttle to the radar plot.

In conjunction with the installation of radar antennas, *Hornet* was fitted with this radar plot, as shown in a December 8, 1941, photograph. This was on the flag bridge level, directly underneath the air plot on the pilothouse level. Note the two lamps on swivel mounts (*to the left*) and the blackboard (*to the right*).

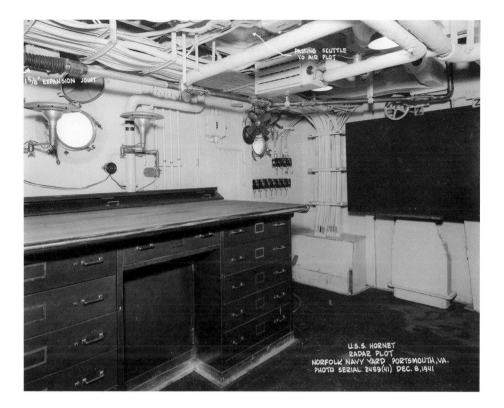

In late February 1942, the *Hornet* was drydocked at Norfolk to ready for transit to its new assignment in the Pacific. In this photograph, dated February 28, 1942, the condition of the carrier's starboard propellers, shafts, and struts is documented.

Under the port outboard propeller, workers are cleaning and repairing the stuffing box for that propeller's shaft. A stuffing box is the fitting through which the propeller shaft exits the hull and enters the water. It contains packing, which excludes seawater from entering the hull.

In the left background, several men are working on the outboard port propeller shaft where it enters the hull. The cavity where the stuffing box has been removed is visible.

During its yard time at the Norfolk Navy Yard in February 1942, the *Hornet* was repainted, this time in Measure 12 (Modified) camouflage. This scheme had the same colors as the standard Measure 12 that the *Hornet* had worn up to this point, but the colors were applied in an irregular pattern, as seen on the island in this image. Some of the alterations made to the island in the February 1942 modernization at Norfolk included omitting the platform for two 36-inch searchlights on the smokestack in favor of a smaller platform with one 36-inch searchlight, and the removal of the pylon that supported a director tub to the port side of the top of the boat crane. This tub now was supported by the ladder frame on the rear of the superstructure. Curtiss SBC-4 Helldivers from Scouting Squadron 8 are lined up on the flight deck.

The island of the *Hornet* is observed from the front at the Norfolk Navy Yard on February 28, 1942. The two Mk. 37 directors now were equipped with Mk. 4 radar; the antennas were mounted on the director roofs. The rangefinder had been removed from above the pilothouse, and a new, curved splinter shield with a curved top for deflecting wind was mounted atop the pilothouse. A Grumman F4F Wildcat is parked in the foreground.

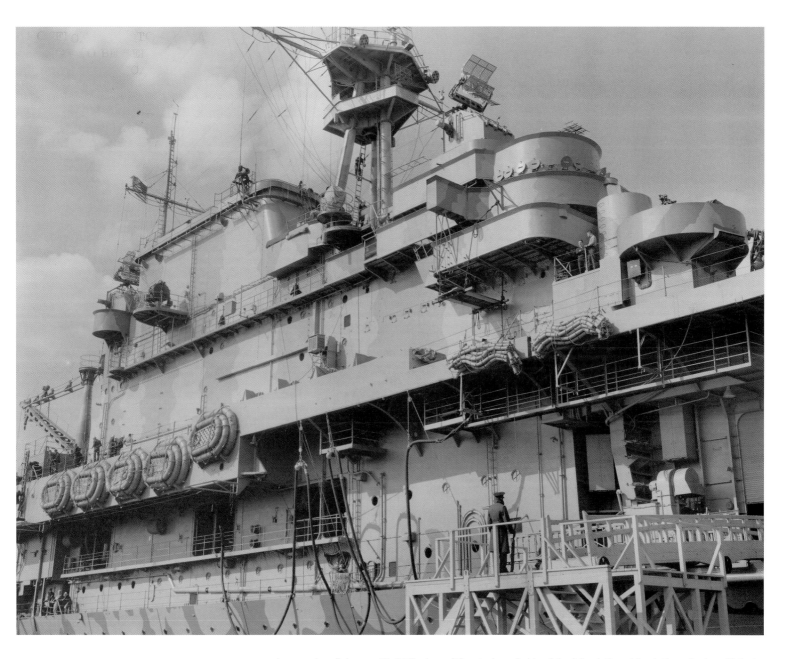

As seen in a February 28, 1942, view of the starboard side of the island, the wide platform for two 36-inch searchlights on this side of the island had been replaced by a narrower platform with one 36-inch searchlight. The boat storage space on the main deck, adjacent to the island, had been replaced by a gallery with four 20 mm guns, and the forward boat crane alongside the island had been removed.

As seen from a perspective farther aft on February 28, 1942, at Norfolk, nested life rafts are stored on the side of the gallery deck. Just forward of the front nest of rafts are recently installed hoses and fittings for accomplishing refueling at sea. The openings below the rafts were intakes for *Hornet*'s boilers.

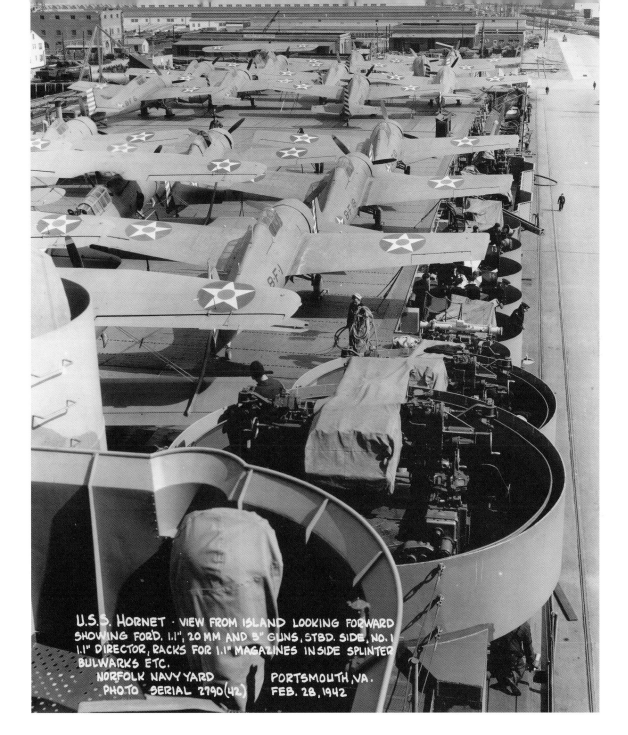

U.S.S. HORNET · VIEW FROM ISLAND LOOKING FORWARD
SHOWING FORD. 1.1", 20 MM AND 5" GUNS, STBD. SIDE, NO. 1
1.1" DIRECTOR, RACKS FOR 1.1" MAGAZINES INSIDE SPLINTER
BULWARKS ETC.
NORFOLK NAVY YARD   PORTSMOUTH, VA.
PHOTO SERIAL 2790(42)   FEB. 28, 1942

As seen from above the forward starboard corner of the flag bridge on February 28, 1942, to the far left is
the tub for the director for the forward 1.1-inch guns. To the right, below the bridge, are the two forward
quad 1.1-inch gun mounts, inside their tub-shaped splinter shields. On the gallery deck are four new tubs,
each with a 20 mm gun mount in it; covers are installed over these mounts. On the flight deck is a mix of
Curtiss SBC-4 Helldivers and Grumman F4F Wildcats.

Some of the *Hornet*'s newly applied Measure 12 (Modified) camouflage scheme is on display in this view of part of the starboard part of the carrier at Norfolk Navy Yard in early 1942.

Hornet is viewed from dockside at Norfolk Navy Yard with F4Fs and SBC-4s embarked. The raised tub for two 20 mm guns on the forecastle was a new addition. On the sponson just forward of the first hangar-deck door, the barrel of a 5-inch/38-caliber gun is visible. Another such gun is to the rear of it on the same sponson. In all, *Hornet* had eight 5-inch/38-caliber guns.

The new splinter shields, or tubs, for 20 mm gun mounts along the gallery deck, and the reinforced framing underneath to support them, are in view. Alongside the forward tub is an outrigger in the retracted position. The outrigger, when swung outward and secured, was used for storing aircraft so that much of the airframe was off the flight deck, thus saving space. This was done by engaging the tailwheel of the plane on the outrigger and pushing the plane backward as far as it would go.

This overall view of the *Hornet* from the port side was taken at Norfolk Navy Yard shortly before the ship departed for its new posting in the Pacific. The carrier would retain this Measure 12 (Modified) camouflage scheme for the remainder of its life.

CHAPTER 3

"Shangri-La": The Doolittle Raid

In early 1942, after the Pearl Harbor attack and the imminent defeat in the Philippines, the United States badly needed a victory, no matter how small or symbolic, for morale and retaliatory purposes. Thus, after feasibility tests in February proved that US Army Air Forces B-25 Mitchell medium bombers could operate from the flight deck of USS *Hornet*, plans went forward for a raid on the Japanese homeland by such planes, to be launched from the *Hornet*. In this photo, Navy blimp L-8 is lowering supplies, including navigators domes for the Mitchells, to the flight deck of the *Hornet* not long after the carrier group, designated Task Force 16, commanded by VAdm. William F. Halsey Jr., departed from San Francisco prior to what would become known as the Doolittle Raid, on April 2, 1942. On the flight deck is one of the B-25B bombers employed in the raid. *Naval History and Heritage Command*

"They came from our secret base at Shangri-La," said President Franklin Roosevelt, responding to a reporter's question as to the origin of the bombers striking Tokyo and five other Japanese cities.

On March 4, the freshly repainted *Hornet* stood out from Norfolk, bound for the West Coast. After transiting the Panama Canal, *Hornet* arrived in San Diego on March 20.

During the brief three-day stay in San Diego, new F4F-4s replaced Fighting 8's F4F-3s, and new SBD-3 Dauntless dive bombers replaced the older biplanes. The next week was spent with carrier qualification training for new pilots, and familiarization with the new aircraft. On March 30, *Hornet* shifted to Alameda, where it took aboard sixteen Army B-25 Mitchell bombers that had arrived from Eglin, Florida, only a few days earlier, flown by a cadre of men who had been training intensely for short takeoffs and low-level bombing. A total of twenty-two bombers had flown west, but six were scrubbed from going aboard owing to mechanical problems. The crews of some of those scrubbed aircraft were taken aboard, however, to serve as backups.

With the bombers aboard, *Hornet* sailed to San Francisco Bay. While what a handful of people knew was going to happen was a secret, having Army bombers loaded onto an aircraft carrier was not in itself a military secret, since Navy aircraft carriers were being extensively used to ferry and deliver army aircraft to the far reaches of the world. So unremarkable was this that no photos have surfaced showing *Hornet* laden with the B-25s in San Francisco Bay.

Hornet and its escorts left San Francisco on April 2, 1942, steaming toward Japan. It rendezvoused with Task Force 16, centered on the *Enterprise*, near Midway. The operational plan was that *Enterprise* would put up the combat air patrol, protecting the task force and scouting, and the ships would move to a point 400 miles off Japan before launching the B-25s. This would allow the bombers adequate range to strike targets in Tokyo and four other cities and then proceed to China, where they would land. In the event the enemy was encountered en route, the B-25s would be pushed overboard, and *Hornet*'s air group would take the deck to join the *Enterprise* airmen in defending the task force.

Steaming through heavy seas in complete radio silence, on April 17, Adm. William "Bull" Halsey, commanding the task force, signaled the destroyers and oilers escorting the ships to stay behind, and the two carriers along with their escorting cruisers plowed ahead, moving closer to Japan and the intended launch date of April 19.

The afternoon of April 17 was filled with taking official photographs of the crews, and a ceremony during which various medals presented to US servicemen by the Japanese government in the past were attached to bombs, so that they could be "returned to sender." The ceremonies and photographs concluded, the bombers were fueled and armed for launch, as the weather deteriorated even further. Waves crashed upon the flight deck, 60 feet above the waterline, and the pace of the ships slowed from 25 to 20 knots.

At 0745 the next morning, the carefully laid launch plan began to unravel when a Japanese picket boat was sighted by Seaman Hubert Gibbons from the escorting cruiser USS *Vincennes*. The Japanese vessel, picket 23 *Nitto Maru*, also spotted the task force and radioed the sighting to Japan. The cruiser *Nashville* (CL-43) opened fire with her 6-inch guns. With the heavy seas bobbing *Nitto Maru*, it took far too many rounds before finally finding their mark and sending the picket to the bottom of the Pacific. Additional Japanese vessels were also sighted, and *Enterprise*'s aircraft engaged *Iwate Maru No. 1*, *Chokyu Maru*, *Asami Maru No. 2*, *Kaijin Maru*, *Chinyo Maru No. 3*, *Eikichi Maru*, *Nagato Maru*, *Nanshin Maru No. 26*, *Kowa Maru*, and *Awata Maru*.

With the element of surprise lost, the decision was made to launch the bombers immediately. While they were 150 miles from the originally planned launch point, the targets in Japan were within the range of the bombers, even if the originally planned landing fields were not. Doolittle's men would launch, strike their targets, and then press on to China in hopes of finding a friendly area to land.

While the picket boats had informed Japan that three US carriers were headed that way, they did not tell them what type of aircraft were aboard. The Japanese, believing that the American fleet was hours away from being able to launch a strike, sent their own fleet in search of the US ships, and they put up no air defense.

Doolittle's men roared over the Japanese mainland, dropping high explosive and incendiary bombs. While the bombing had minimal tactical effect, strategically the impact was huge. Japanese civilian morale was shaken, the Japanese military leadership was embarrassed, and concerns about additional strikes brought a redeployment of Japanese forces for months, with units previously earmarked for offensive operations instead relegated to the defense of the home islands.

While the Japanese used torture to extract from prisoners the origin of the raid, in the US the details remained secret for over a year.

As for the Doolittle Raiders, one aircraft landed safely in Russia, where the crew was interned for over a year and the aircraft was confiscated. All fifteen of the other bombers reached China, where eight of the crewmen were captured by the Japanese, with three of these men subsequently executed following mock trials. Three additional men were killed in action. In Japan, about fifty people were killed and 400 injured by the bombing raids, these being both military and civilian. By far the worst casualties were in China, where an estimated 10,000 people were killed in reprisals for their aid to the Americans.

Seven of the sixteen B-25Bs for the Doolittle Raid are spotted on the flight deck of USS *Hornet* (CV-8) during the transit west from San Francisco to Japanese waters in April 1942. Also on deck are two Navy SBD Dauntless dive-bombers. The destroyer USS *Gwin* (DD-433) and, farther to the rear, the cruiser USS *Nashville* (CL-43) are escorting the *Hornet*. Note the quad 1.1-inch and 20 mm gun mounts on the gallery. *National Museum of the United States Air Force*

The engine is run up on one of the three Dauntless dive bombers visible parked among the Army bombers in this view of *Hornet*'s deck. *Hornet*'s own aircraft were kept in top shape, since if need be, the Army aircraft would be pushed over the side so *Hornet* could defend herself. *National Museum of Naval Aviation*

In a photograph taken from the catwalk along the port side of the smokestack of the *Hornet*, with the primary fly control booth with its rectangular windows in the background, B-25Bs are secured to the flight deck. Fake machine gun barrels were attached to the tails of these aircraft, and a pair of them may be seen on the second bomber. To the front of these planes, the palisades (a row of hinged slats that acted as a windbreak when raised) are visible. *Naval History and Heritage Command*

Two Army B-25Bs, including serial number 40-2282 (*to the right*), piloted by 1st Lt. Everett W. Holstrom, are secured to the flight deck of the *Hornet*. The crews for the Doolittle Raid were drawn from the 17th Bombardment Group (Medium). *Naval History and Heritage Command*

This photo, taken on April 18, 1942, a companion image to the preceding one, was taken farther forward on the catwalk. The portside flag bag is to the far right. To the port side of the searchlight and forward of it, the shape of a pelorus, an optical instrument on a pedestal for taking bearings on distant landmarks, can be made out. This was a recent addition to the top of the pri-fly booth, which is an optical instrument on a pedestal for taking bearings on distant landmarks.

North American B-25B medium bombers assigned to Doolittle's force are seen from the island of the *Hornet*. The closest bomber is serial number 40-2203, piloted by 2nd Lt. Harold F. Watson. *Naval History and Heritage Command*

B-25Bs are viewed close-up, tethered to the flight deck of the *Hornet* en route to the raid on Tokyo and environs. For aircraft of this size, it was critical to secure them as firmly as possible to the flight deck. The rope stays are attached to the tie-down strips running laterally across the deck. *Naval History and Heritage Command*

The imitation machine gun barrels installed on the clear domes on the tails of B-25Bs destined for the Tokyo raid were intended to dissuade enemy fighter pilots from approaching the vulnerable rears of the planes. "Slots" were painted on the clear domes to further the illusion of a tail turret. *Naval History and Heritage Command*

B-25B Mitchells spotted on the flight deck of USS *Hornet* en route to their launching point include serial number 40-2250, piloted by 1st Lt. Richard O. Joyce.

This B-25B spotted on the aft end of the flight deck of the *Hornet* presumably was the number 16 plane, serial number 40-2268, nicknamed "Bat out of Hell." Note the safety rail along the rear of the flight deck, in the form of a chain supported by stanchions. *Naval History and Heritage Command*

Some of the Doolittle Raid B-25Bs had nicknames. This one was "Hari Kari-er," serial number 40-2249, piloted by Capt. C. Ross Greening. It featured nose art of a winged nude woman holding a bomb in her hands. Gunners on this bomber claimed two kills of Japanese fighter planes during the raid. *Naval History and Heritage Command*

Army Air Forces and Navy officers confer on the flight deck of USS *Hornet* prior to the launching of the Doolittle Raid. To the right is a B-25B, serial number 40-2242, which was the number 8 plane, piloted by Capt. Edward J. York. *Naval History and Heritage Command*

Crewmen of the *Hornet* standing around the 36-inch searchlight on the port side of the smokestack survey the activities on the flight deck in preparation for the Doolittle Raid. The nearest plane, serial number 40-2261, was nicknamed "Ruptured Duck" and was piloted by 1st Lt. Ted W. Lawson, who would write an account of the raid, *Thirty Seconds over Tokyo. Naval History and Heritage Command*

VAN JOHNSON

Doolittle is wiring Japanese medals, donated by US Navy veterans, to the fin of a 500-pound bomb, for symbolic return to their country of origin.

The several Japanese medals affixed to the bomb are depicted in close-up.

Crewmen of Doolittle's force are loading .50-caliber ammunition into magazines on the flight deck of USS *Hornet* in preparation for the raid on Tokyo. This was an operation typically undertaken on or very close to the date of a combat mission. *Naval History and Heritage Command*

Early on the morning of April 18, 1942, some 650 nautical miles from Japan, and far short of optimal launching range, Task Force 16 was discovered and reported by a Japanese picket boat, *Nitto Maru*. This forced Adm. Halsey to order the launching of Doolittle's B-25Bs. The task force encountered other picket boats before clearing the area. Shown here is one of the escort ships, the light cruiser USS *Nashville* (CL-43), shelling a Japanese craft. *Naval History and Heritage Command*

A 500-pound bomb on a bomb truck has been brought up to the main deck of the *Hornet* on the aft bomb elevator, alongside the island, for loading into one of the Doolittle Raiders' B-25Bs.

The loading of .50-caliber ammo magazines for the Doolittle B-25Bs is observed from the searchlight platform on the port side of the smokestack. In the right background, several men are standing around the well of a bomb elevator. *Naval History and Heritage Command*

With the wing of a B-25B to the right and the island of the *Hornet* in the background, members of the Doolittle Raiders are loading .50-caliber ammunition into metal magazines. Some of the crewmen of the carrier are watching the procedure with interest.

The USS *Hornet* bucks large waves during Task Force 16's approach to Japan in April 1942. The photo was taken from the cruiser USS *Salt Lake City* (CA-25).

The B-25Bs are running up their engines in preparation for takeoff on the famed Tokyo raid of April 18, 1942. The aircraft have been spotted as far aft as possible on the flight deck to allow room for takeoff runs. The number 5 plane, serial number 40-2283, is to the far right; farther aft are planes number 6 to 16.

Officers and members of the crew of USS *Hornet* watch intently from the level above the pilothouse as a B-25B lifts off the flight deck. The first plane to take off was Doolittle's, serial number 40-2344, which lifted off the deck at 0820. *National Museum of the United States Air Force*

In one of the iconic photographs of World War II, a North American B-25B takes to the air from USS *Hornet*. In the foreground is the forward port searchlight platform; below it is pri-fly. *National Museum of the United States Air Force*

A B-25B gains altitude to the right after taking off from the *Hornet*. The Measure 12 (Modified) camouflage of the ship is easily discernible. *National Museum of the United States Air Force*

A B-25B is being readied for launching while the plane aft of it is warming its engines. The sea was quite rough during the takeoffs for the Doolittle Raid. *Naval History and Heritage Command*

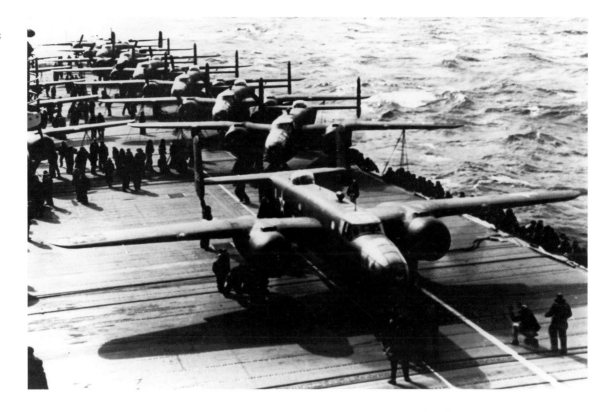

The launch officer on the *Hornet* (*right*) prepares to drop his checkered flag to signal the pilot of the B-25B to commence takeoff. It took almost one hour, from 0820 to 0919, to launch all sixteen bombers. *National Museum of the United States Air Force*

A B-25B is poised for takeoff. The flight deck was wet, since large waves occasionally crashed over the *Hornet*'s flight deck.

This photograph, taken from the level above the pilothouse, shows a B-25B preparing for takeoff, with only three or four bombers remaining behind it on the flight deck. To the left is the ship's smokestack and port 36-inch searchlight. *Naval History and Heritage Command*

This rare photograph shows one of the Doolittle Raiders' B-25Bs about to launch from USS *Hornet*. It was taken from the port catwalk and depicts the approximate midpoint of the hourlong launchings. About a half-dozen B-25Bs remain on the after part of the flight deck, awaiting their turns to launch.

The only surviving strike photos of the Doolittle Raid were taken on 1st Lt. Edgar E. McElroy's B-25B, serial number 40-2247. This aircraft's target was the Imperial Japanese Navy base at Yokosuka, in the southwestern part of Tokyo Bay. This photograph was taken over or near that naval base. *National Museum of the United States Air Force*

Another photo snapped from McElroy's B-25B shows the shoreline near Yokosuka Naval Base. At an altitude of 1,500 feet, this plane bombed dock facilities at the base, reportedly destroying a large crane, damaging the carrier *Ryuho* in drydock, and causing other destruction. *National Museum of the United States Air Force*

After the B-25Bs of the Doolittle Raid attacked their targets in Japan, their next task was to try to escape to airfields in parts of China not occupied by the Japanese. In reality, all but one of the planes were forced to crash-land or ditch in the ocean; the one plane that landed did so in the Soviet Union, and the crew was interned there. Doolittle and his crew bailed out of their plane over China, and he is shown here sitting next to the wreckage of his plane. *National Museum of the United States Air Force*

Madame Chiang Kai-shek, the wife of Generalissimo Chiang Kai-shek, reads the citation after the presentation of the Military Order of China to Jimmy Doolittle, *second from right*, and Col. John A. Hilger, *right*, commander of plane number 14 in the Doolittle Raid. *National Museum of the United States Air Force*

Once the Japanese learned that most of the crews of the Doolittle Raid had made their way to China, reprisals were harsh, with the Japanese reportedly killing many civilians and extending their area of occupation in China. Two of the American crews were captured by the Japanese in China. Here, a blindfolded Lt. Robert Hite, copilot of B-25B number 16, is being led by his captors from a transport plane. He survived captivity, but the Japanese executed three of the airmen. *National Museum of the United States Air Force*

The Japanese captured eight members of the Doolittle Raiders, including Crew No. 16, shown here with their guards. These crewmen are in the back row of the photo and are, *left to right*, Cpl. Jacob DeShazer, Sgt. Harold A. Spatz, Lt. Robert L. Hite, plane commander Lt. William G. Farrow, and Lt. George Barr. *National Museum of the United States Air Force*

Crewmen on USS *Hornet* scramble to secure a Grumman F4F Wildcat that has crashed onto the gallery during a landing gone wrong, following a patrol mission. The original label of the image states that it was taken on April 18, 1942, but since the logbook of the *Hornet* for that date mentions no such crashes, it is likely this event happened during Task Force 16's return voyage from the raid on Tokyo.

After arriving at Pearl Harbor one week after launching the Doolittle Raid, the *Hornet* was quickly turned around, and on April 28, 1942, it was dispatched to the Coral Sea. This photo, though sometimes described as showing the *Hornet* upon her arrival at Pearl Harbor after the Doolittle Raid, more likely shows the carrier departing from Pearl for the Coral Sea on April 28, since the carrier is heading away from Oahu rather than approaching it. Escorting the *Hornet* are PT-28 and PT-29.

CHAPTER 4
A Fighter to the End

On May 15, 1942, USS *Hornet* is steaming in the South Pacific. It arrived in the Coral Sea too late by one week to participate in that battle. On the day after this photo was taken, the carrier was ordered back to Pearl Harbor to be put into condition for an operation that proved to be a decisive one in the struggle for the Pacific: the Battle of Midway. *National Museum of Naval Aviation*

When the last of the B-25s, Lt. William Farrow's "Bat out of Hell," had left *Hornet*'s deck, Halsey swung the task force around and hurried toward Pearl Harbor, arriving at the port a week later. After only a few days in port, on April 30, *Hornet* left Pearl Harbor to join *Lexington* (CV-2) and *Yorktown* (CV-5) at the Battle of Coral Sea, but the battle was over before *Hornet* arrived. *Hornet* returned to Pearl, only to steam out again two days later, bound for Midway.

Hornet itself was unscathed in this battle, which cost the Japanese four aircraft carriers and a cruiser and led to the sinking of *Hornet*'s sister ship *Yorktown*. *Hornet* was not without its loss, since Torpedo Squadron 8, flying from its decks, was wiped out during the battle while attacking the Japanese fleet. Of the thirty men, only Ens. George Gay, pilot of one of the TBDs (Torpedo Bombers Douglas), survived. He had been shot down right in the middle of the Japanese fleet, remarkably surviving not only the crash but also the annihilation of the Japanese carriers just feet from him, and being picked up later by a US Navy PBY (Patrol Bomber Y, the "Y" being a code assigned to its manufacturer Consolidated) thirty hours later. The rest of the squadron's pilots and gunners / radio operators were lost.

Hornet returned to Pearl Harbor for shipyard work, her first since arriving in the Pacific, and for training with her rebuilt air group. She left Pearl on August 17, 1942, only to find a month later that she was the only operational US aircraft carrier in the Pacific. *Wasp* (CV-7) was sunk on September 15, *Enterprise* had sustained bomb damage on August 24, and *Saratoga* (CV-3) had suffered torpedo damage a week later.

On September 24, *Hornet*, along with the repaired *Enterprise*, set out to intercept a Japanese force headed for Guadalcanal. The clash of forces occurred on October 26, in what is known as the Battle of Santa Cruz. *Hornet* launched aircraft that struck the carrier *Shōkaku* and the cruiser *Chikuma*, causing severe damage to both. The Japanese, having sighted the US force, launched their own attack. With *Enterprise* and its escorts hidden by a rain squall, *Hornet* bore the brunt of the Japanese attack. Twenty Japanese torpedo planes and sixteen dive bombers pressed home their attacks on *Hornet*, with three bombs hitting the carrier in rapid succession, and less than two minutes later a Japanese bomber, damaged by antiaircraft fire, deliberately crashed into *Hornet*'s superstructure, spreading burning gasoline.

One minute after the first bomb hit *Hornet*, the first torpedo hit the ship, followed four minutes later by a second. Ablaze, and with her engines stopped by the torpedoes, *Hornet* began to slow, when yet another Japanese bomber purposefully crashed into the ship.

Assisted by escorting destroyers who sprayed water on the ship, the fires were brought under control, and a tow line was rigged to the cruiser *Northampton* (CA-26). After the first tow line parted, a heavier line was rigged and the towing operation begun again, while at the same time, damage control teams and *Hornet*'s engineering staff worked at restoring the ship's own power. Considerable progress had been made, when about forty minutes after beginning the successful tow, a second wave of Japanese aircraft arrived, causing towing efforts to be abandoned. Seven Japanese aircraft launched torpedoes, six of which missed, but the seventh struck amidships, again disabling the engineering spaces and causing heavy flooding. The order was passed to abandon ship, and while doing so yet another wave of Japanese attackers arrived, this time hitting the ship with another bomb.

With Japanese surface ships rapidly approaching, and *Hornet* heavily damaged, the order was given to scuttle the carrier. Escorting destroyers fired multiple torpedoes and over 400 rounds of 5-inch shells at the hulk, which, although ablaze, refused to sink. With the Japanese only twenty minutes away, the destroyers gave up, leaving *Hornet* adrift. At 22:20 the Japanese ships arrived, and Imperial Japanese Navy destroyers *Makigumo* and *Akigumo* fired four torpedoes at the ship. At 01:35 the next morning, *Hornet* sank beneath the waves of the Pacific.

Sailors on tow tractors at Naval Air Station Ford Island watch as USS *Hornet* steams past upon its return to Pearl Harbor from the Coral Sea on May 26, 1942. There, it would be quickly serviced and reprovisioned before being dispatched to Midway on May 28. The paint on the ship has suffered considerable wear, and this is most apparent on the hull, above the boot topping.

USS *Hornet* is viewed from directly abeam as it makes its way through the waters of Pearl Harbor, assisted by the harbor tug *Nokomis* (YT-142) on May 26, 1942. The *Hornet*'s air group had flown off the carrier before entering Pearl Harbor and had proceeded to the Marine base at Ewa until the ship returned to sea.

Harbor tugs are maneuvering the *Hornet* toward its berth alongside Ford Island at Pearl Harbor on May 26, 1942. During the two days the carrier was in port, the liberty was canceled for the crew of *Hornet* for security reasons, since the Americans had decoded Japanese messages detailing their plans for an offensive against the Midway Islands, and the fleet was being readied for a rapid advance to meet and attempt to surprise the Japanese.

USS *Hornet* is being moored to its berth alongside Ford Island on May 26, 1942. The extent of the erosion of the camouflage paint above the boot topping is readily apparent. A very small number "8," the carrier's number, is painted in white on the bow, aft of the anchor and above the hawser.

In an undated photo thought to have been taken during or around the time of the Battle of Midway in early June 1942, a Douglas SBD Dauntless dive-bomber attempting a landing seems to be nearly out of control, with its wings canted and positioned too far to the port side of the flight deck. *National Museum of Naval Aviation*

A Douglas SBD-3 Dauntless dive-bomber is about to recover on USS *Hornet* during or around the time of the Battle of Midway. At the commencement of that battle on June 4, 1942, the *Hornet* had two squadrons equipped with SBD-3s, numbering nineteen planes each: Scouting Squadron 8 (VS-8) and Bombing Squadron 8. *National Museum of Naval Aviation*

As seen from alongside the forward end of the island, an SBD-3 has just recovered on *Hornet*'s flight deck, and another SBD-3 is about to land. The deck crewmen are wearing full battle gear, suggesting that the photo was taken during the Battle of Midway. *National Museum of Naval Aviation*

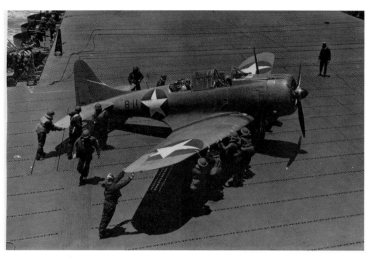

Airedales, as deck crewmen are nicknamed, are maneuvering the number 11 SBD-3 from VB-8 on the flight deck of the *Hornet* in June 1942, presumably during the Battle of Midway. These sailors are wearing a mix of the old M1917 helmets and the newer M1 helmets. The airedale to the far left is standing on a torpedo elevator. *National Museum of Naval Aviation*

Although the original Navy caption for this photo states that it was taken on August 21, 1942, this photo of USS *Hornet* being escorted by the light cruiser USS *Atlanta* (CL-51) is now believed to have been taken during the Battle of Midway. Aircraft are spotted on the flight deck from the island aft, and at least one plane is visible to the front of the island.

Torpedo Squadron 8 (VT-8), embarked on USS *Hornet*, was destroyed on the first day of the Battle of Midway, June 4, 1942. Attacking the Japanese fleet in obsolete Douglas TBD Devastator torpedo bombers, the fifteen planes were shot down one by one before they could inflict any damage on the enemy. Only one of the squadron members who flew on that mission, Ens. George Gay, survived the slaughter, but the sacrifice of Torpedo 8 set the stage for great success for the following waves of USN dive-bombers. Pilots of VT-8 gathered for a group portrait before the battle. They are, *standing, left to right*: Owens, Fayle, Squadron Commander Lt. Cdr. John Waldron, R. A. Moore, J. M. Moore, Evans, Teats, and Campbell; and, *kneeling, left to right*: Ellison, Kenyon, Gray, Gay, Woodson, Creamer, and Miles. *Naval History and Heritage Command*

ENCLOSURE (A) to HORNET
Conf.Ltr. CV8/A9/A16-3
Serial ___ 04.
Photograph taken of plane
as it was firing.

June 4, 1942, was a very tragic day for USS *Hornet*. In addition to the destruction of Torpedo 8, five members of the *Hornet*'s crew were killed and twenty were wounded when a wounded F4F-4 Wildcat pilot, Ens. Daniel Sheedy, from VF-3 on USS *Yorktown* (CV-5), accidentally fired the fighter's .50-caliber machine guns while making an emergency landing on *Hornet*. According to the official report, the accident was the result of the pilot's wounds and battle damage to the machine gun safety system. The Wildcat is seen here careening on the deck with its .50-caliber machine guns firing.
National Archives / San Bruno

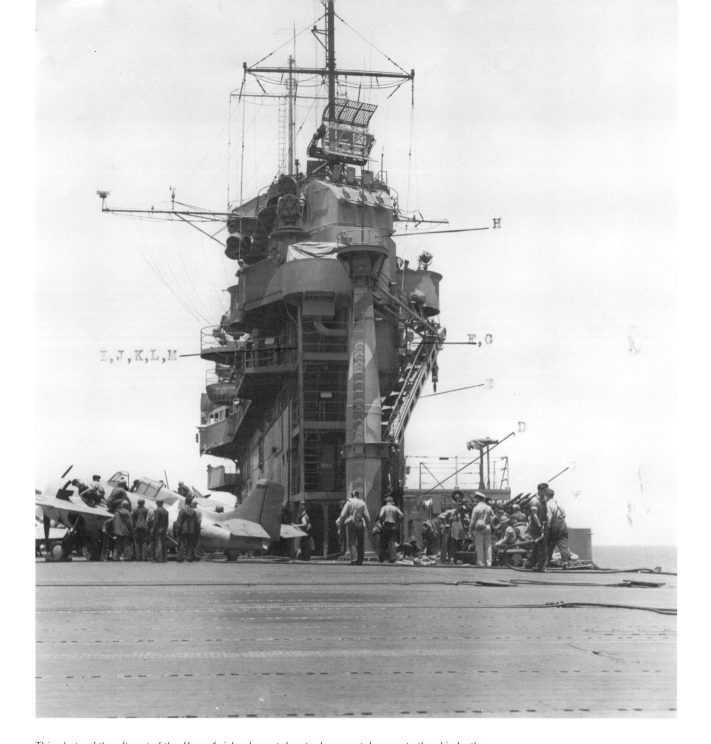

This photo of the aft part of the *Hornet*'s island was taken to document damage to the ship by the .50-caliber machine guns of Ens. Sheedy's F4F-4 on June 4, 1942. The slugs (steel jacketed, with every third round a tracer) damaged the number 3 1.1-inch gun mount and splinter shield, the aircraft crane, the starboard 36-inch searchlight, the secondary control station, and other structures on the island.
National Archives / San Bruno

After the Battle of Midway, USS *Hornet* returned to Pearl Harbor, where it underwent several months of badly needed repairs and maintenance. Among other tasks performed during that time, the Measure 12 (Modified) camouflage paint was renewed on the carrier, and the SC radar was removed and replaced by a CXAM radar, with a larger antenna, salvaged from the wreckage of the battleship USS *California* at Pearl Harbor. The number of 20 mm guns was increased from twenty-four to thirty-eight, and a fifth quad 1.1-inch gun mount was installed on the bow. The *Hornet* is seen here from her aft starboard quarter sometime during August 1942 at Pearl Harbor.

After receiving repairs and modernization at Pearl Harbor, the *Hornet* departed for the South Pacific on August 17, 1942. It supported Allied operations in the Solomon Islands Campaign. On the morning of October 26, 1942, while operating to intercept the Japanese Combined Fleet near the Santa Cruz Islands, *Hornet* was assaulted by Japanese dive-bombers and torpedo bombers. First, the *Hornet* took a bomb hit just starboard of the centerline of the flight deck, and then, moments later, a damaged, flaming Val dive-bomber crashed into the smokestack, also destroying the signal bridge, creating a hole in the flight deck, and raining debris and flames on the sailors in the vicinity. In this photo, *Hornet* is heeling hard to starboard before the first attack on October 26.

A photographer on USS *Pensacola* captured this shot of the Val dive-bomber crashing and exploding on USS *Hornet*. The plane was carrying one 551-pound and two 132-pound bombs, which added to the destruction. Antiaircraft bursts from *Hornet* and its escorts dot the sky overhead.

Smoke is pouring through the flight deck after a bomb struck the *Hornet*. During the morning attack, the carrier also sustained two torpedo hits, and another Japanese aircraft, a Kate torpedo bomber, deliberately crashed into the port side of the forecastle, plowing into the ship as far as the hangar deck and creating a fire that threatened to engulf the forward part of the carrier. Engines and electrical systems damaged, the carrier came to a stop, unable to maneuver or launch or recover aircraft.

The *Hornet* is viewed from its port side as it burns, with flames visible alongside her upper superstructure, and listing to the starboard.

Dead in the water, the *Hornet* is viewed off its port bow from USS *Anderson* during the morning attack during the Battle of the Santa Cruz Islands on October 26, 1942. The heavy black smoke is issuing from the hangar deck, where fires were started by the second aircraft hit.

While the bombs and suicide planes caused sufficient havoc on the *Hornet*, it was torpedo strikes that created a real crisis, placing the forward engine room out of commission and creating other destruction. This photograph was taken while Japanese aircraft were launching torpedoes at USS *Hornet*. One of the planes is visible above the aft part of the carrier. Smoke and spray are rising from where one of two torpedoes struck the ship during the morning attack.

While smoke was still boiling from the interior of the ship, a photographer ventured close enough to the superstructure to take this harrowing view of the damage caused to the smokestack (*right*), the foretop, and the signal bridge, adjacent to the bottom of the tripod mast.

Crewmen struggle valiantly to extinguish the fires on USS *Hornet* following the morning attack on October 26, 1942. To the upper right is the pri-fly.

Thick smoke pours from the *Hornet* after the morning attack. While the carrier was enduring this ordeal, its air group was attacking the Japanese fleet, managing to heavily damage the carrier *Shokaku* and the cruiser *Chikuma*. After these attacks, the air group was forced to recover on the carrier *Enterprise*.

Smoke is billowing out of USS *Hornet* as destroyers from its escort screen are coming alongside following the first attack on the morning of October 26. For a while, the fires on the carrier threatened to destroy it and its crew.

Hornet is dead in the water and still smoking after the first attack on the morning of October 26, 1942. Many crewmen are along the port side of the flight deck, and dozens of knotted lines have been lowered from the flight deck for the use of the crew should the order be given to abandon ship.

A photographer on the destroyer USS *Russell* (DD-414) took this image of the heavily listing and still-smoking *Hornet* as the destroyer approached the carrier to render aid. The recently installed CXAM radar antenna is visible on the foretop.

This remarkable, previously unpublished photo shows the full length of the *Hornet* from the port side, with USS *Russell* alongside, rendering aid after the morning attacks in the Battle of Santa Cruz. Hundreds of crewmen are on the deck of the carrier, since during this time frame it was expected that the order to abandon ship might be issued. To the front of *Russell*'s superstructure is the forward port 5-inch/38-caliber gun gallery; it was just forward of that gallery that the second suicide plane struck the carrier.

After the morning attacks on October 26, the destroyers *Russell* and *Morris* (DD-417) moved in close alongside the *Hornet* to render any assistance possible. Here, the *Russell* moves in toward *Hornet*'s port bow. When the *Russell* was closer, a large swell slammed the destroyer against the carrier, knocking a depth charge loose from its rack and into the ocean; fortunately, it failed to detonate.

Russell stands by the *Hornet* while another destroyer of the carrier's screening force passes by. Japanese aircraft are beginning to attack again, and antiaircraft fire has broken out.

A photographer on USS *Russell* took this photo of the *Hornet* as the destroyer came alongside the carrier's port beam. The wounded were passed from the *Hornet* to the *Russell* for evacuation, and the *Russell* passed over fire hoses for combating the fires on the *Hornet*.

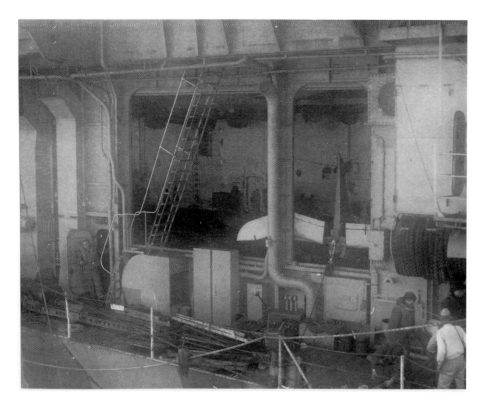

A photograph taken from USS *Russell* shows a portion of the port side of the hull of the *Hornet* along the hangar deck between frames 145 and 155. Inside the roller-door opening to the left is the tail of an aircraft that evidently had been slammed into this awkward position by the force of explosions. The tail landing gear is hooked over the doorsill, the horizontal stabilizers have been jammed, upright, against the sides of the door, and the rudder is missing from the vertical fin.

The hangar deck amidships and the island are viewed from the port side in another photo taken from USS *Russell*. Within an hour of the attack, all fires on the *Hornet* were under control; all fires were out an hour after that. While the *Russell* was alongside the *Hornet*, heavy swells frequently slammed the destroyer against the much-larger carrier, causing damage to *Russell*'s upper works and the loss of its starboard anchor. Note the devastation to the upper forward part of the smokestack, where the first Japanese suicide plane crashed.

An aerial photographer took this view of the *Hornet* after most or all of the fires onboard were brought under control, around late morning on October 26. On its port quarter is USS *Russell*. One of the bomb entry holes is on the starboard side of the flight deck, midway between the aft ramp of the deck and the island. Less visible are the points where the two torpedoes struck the starboard side of the hull during the morning attack; one detonated below the waterline, a few frames aft of the bomb entry hole seen in this photo, while the other one struck below the crane, aft of the island.

With the *Hornet* lying dead in the water, an attempt was made to tow it from the area, employing the heavy cruiser USS *Northampton* (CA-26), as seen here. The attempt was a failure for various reasons: the tow cable was insufficient for the mass of the carrier, and the *Hornet*'s rudder was jammed at an angle of 30 degrees, making it impossible to keep the ship aligned with *Northampton*. After only twenty minutes, the tow cable broke, but *Northampton*, after much effort by the crews of both ships, was able to resume towing the *Hornet* by using one of the carrier's own 2-inch tow cables. Finally, *Northampton* was forced to terminate the tow when the Japanese mounted a new attack on the late afternoon of October 26.

This previously unpublished photo was taken from USS *Northampton* as that ship maneuvered to the front of the *Hornet* to take it under tow for the second time during the Battle of Santa Cruz. While this action was going on, the engineering department in the *Hornet* was valiantly attempting to get the remaining engines working, sometimes working in heat of up to 140 degrees Fahrenheit in the machinery spaces.

As photographed from the *Northampton*, sailors aboard the *Hornet* are preparing to receive a tow line from the *Northampton*. It was hoped that the cruiser could tow the crippled aircraft carrier out of the danger zone. The location where the second Japanese suicide plane crashed into the *Hornet* is just forward of and below the platform with the two 5-inch/38-caliber guns, at the center of the photo.

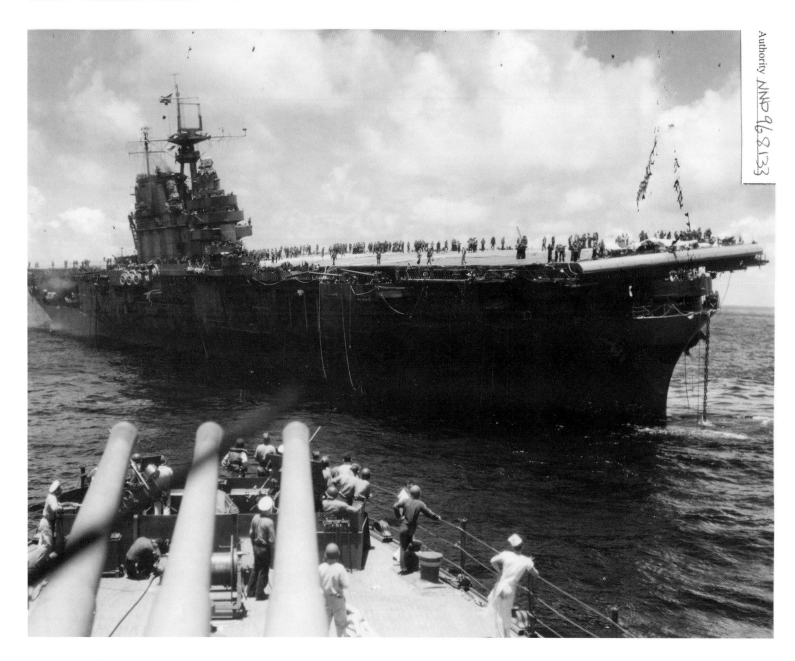

Crewmen of USS *Northampton* stand by on the fantail as preparations are being made to receive a new, thicker (2-inch) tow cable from USS *Hornet*. Smoke is still issuing from the hull of the stricken carrier, aft of the island.

Crewmen on the *Northampton* haul on a 2-inch tow cable, the other end of which is secured to the *Hornet*, during the second attempt to tow the carrier. The destroyer *Russell* is visible along the port side of the *Hornet*. Visible on the forecastle is the forward quad 1.1-inch gun mount, installed after the Battle of Midway, replacing two 20 mm guns in that position. The splinter shield for that mount was also new, its face being fabricated from flat, welded plates, in contrast to the earlier, curved splinter shield.

In a previously unpublished photo, the *Hornet* is viewed from the *Northampton* as the cruiser begins to take the massive carrier under tow for the second time on the afternoon of October 26, 1942. The sheeting rigged over the forward end of the flight deck was to provide shade for wounded sailors.

During the renewed attack on *Hornet* in the late afternoon of October 26, a torpedo dropped by a Kate torpedo bomber has just splashed into the water (*to the far right*), while an aircraft flies over the carrier. Three Kates launched torpedoes against the *Hornet* during the afternoon attack: one torpedo sank, another struck the carrier but was a dud, and the third one detonated on the starboard side at frame 115, with devastating effect.

USS *Hornet* is listing badly to starboard after the afternoon attack. At that point, full efforts were undertaken to abandon ship.

The *Hornet* is viewed at a distance after being abandoned. The carrier at this time was listing 26 degrees.

The carrier is viewed from a closer perspective after being abandoned.

Abandoned and adrift, *Hornet* continues to list as antiaircraft bursts from other ships dot the sky. Late in the day of October 26, the destroyers *Anderson* and *Mustin* attempted to sink the carrier, lest the Japanese capture her, but despite shooting nine torpedoes and almost 400 rounds of 5-inch shells at the ship, she failed to sink. That night, after US forces had cleared the area, Japanese destroyers fired four more torpedoes into *Hornet*, and at 0135 on October 27, she finally went under the waves.